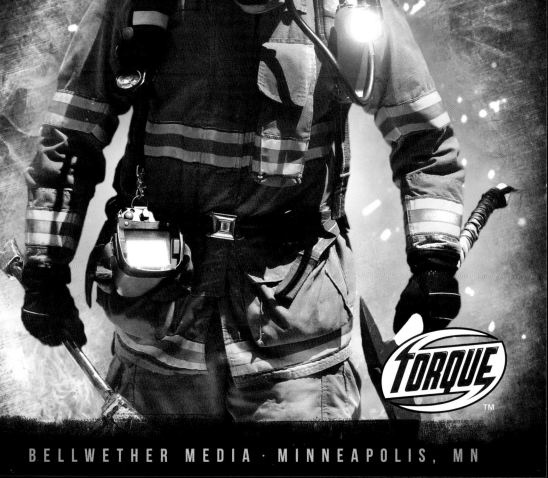

FIREFIGHTER

BY CHRIS BOWMAN

TORQUE™

BELLWETHER MEDIA · MINNEAPOLIS, MN

Are you ready to take it to the extreme?
Torque books thrust you into the action-packed world
of sports, vehicles, mystery, and adventure. These books
may include dirt, smoke, fire, and dangerous stunts.
WARNING: read at your own risk.

Library of Congress Cataloging-in-Publication Data

Bowman, Chris, 1990- author.
 Firefighter / by Chris Bowman.
    pages cm. -- (Torque: Dangerous Jobs)
 Summary: "Engaging images accompany information about firefighters. The combination of high-interest
subject matter and light text is intended for students in grades 3 through 7"-- Provided by publisher.
 Audience: Ages 7-12.
 Audience: Grades 3 to 7.
 Includes bibliographical references and index.
 ISBN 978-1-62617-110-7 (hardcover : alk. paper)
 1. Fire fighters--Juvenile literature. 2. Fire extinction--Juvenile literature. I. Title. II. Title: Fire fighter. III.
Series: Dangerous jobs (Minneapolis, Minn.)
 HD8039.F5B69 2014
 363.37092--dc23
                                  2013050082

This edition first published in 2015 by Bellwether Media, Inc.

Printed in the United States of America, North Mankato, MN.

TABLE OF CONTENTS

CHAPTER 1

FIRE!

A group of firefighters is relaxing at the station. Suddenly, a call comes in. There is a house on fire! The firefighters rush to put on their gear and get to the fire truck. They race to the scene. They are told there is still a man inside!

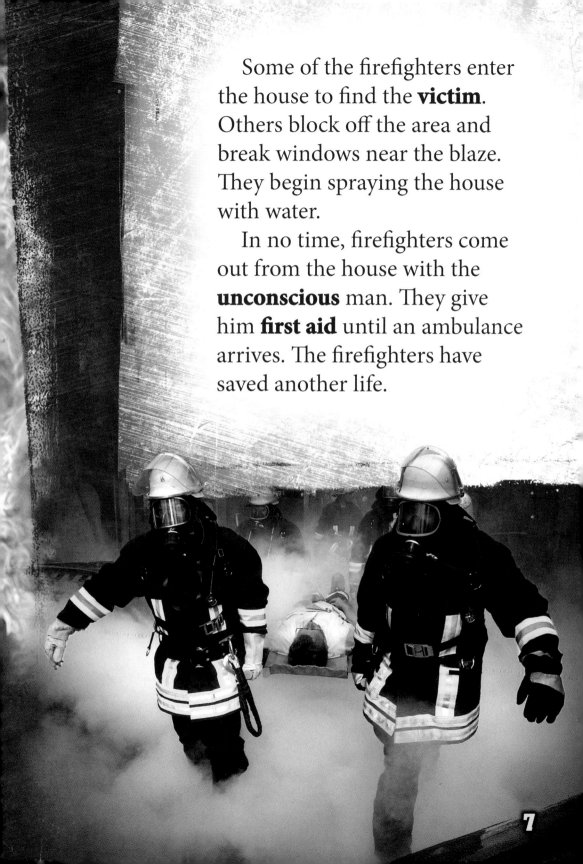

Some of the firefighters enter the house to find the **victim**. Others block off the area and break windows near the blaze. They begin spraying the house with water.

In no time, firefighters come out from the house with the **unconscious** man. They give him **first aid** until an ambulance arrives. The firefighters have saved another life.

CHAPTER 2

FIREFIGHTERS

Firefighters are skilled rescue workers. They are trained to put out fires and save people from dangerous situations. Firefighters are also called to medical emergencies, **natural disasters**, and car accidents. They are often the first people to arrive at the scene of an emergency.

Pass the Bucket

American firefighting began in 1648. The first firefighters formed "bucket brigades." They lined up and passed buckets of water to one another. This water was then used to put out the fire.

New firefighters are checked to make sure they are physically, medically, and mentally fit. They must also pass a written test. Then they can join a department as either a **volunteer** or a **career firefighter**. They complete training programs to learn firefighting skills. Many firefighters have already studied **fire science** in college. At the end of training, all firefighters know emergency medicine and first aid.

Volunteer Heroes

Most firefighters in the United States are volunteers. Many of these brave men and women are not paid for the work they do. Others receive just a small amount of money.

On the job, firefighters put out fires in homes, businesses, and even nature. Their main goal is to keep everyone safe. When they are not out on a call, firefighters teach their communities about fire safety. Many give talks at schools. They also **inspect** old buildings to make sure they are safe.

Firefighter Tasks: RECEO-VS

Rescue:	Remove any known victims from the building
Exposures:	Limit the places the fire can spread
Confinement:	Keep the fire from spreading
Extinguish:	Put the fire out
Overhaul:	Make sure the fire will not start again

If possible, firefighters also complete these steps:

Ventilate:	Allow smoke and heat to escape
Salvage:	Save other property from fire, smoke, or water damage

Firefighters care for victims of an emergency until ambulances arrive. At big emergencies, firefighters may have to stay at the scene for many hours. They switch between duties such as caring for people and battling the fire.

CHAPTER 3

DANGER!

Firefighters face many dangers at work. They might get trapped in a burning building. Breathing in smoke or suffering burns can be deadly. Falling objects can crush them. Floors and stairs might **collapse** under them. They can get injuries from lifting heavy equipment.

Nice Threads

Firefighters' jackets and pants are made to handle temperatures up to 1200 degrees Fahrenheit (650 degrees Celsius). All of their clothes are covered in shiny stripes. This helps other firefighters see them in smoky and dark conditions.

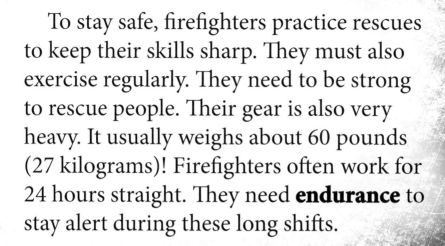

To stay safe, firefighters practice rescues to keep their skills sharp. They must also exercise regularly. They need to be strong to rescue people. Their gear is also very heavy. It usually weighs about 60 pounds (27 kilograms)! Firefighters often work for 24 hours straight. They need **endurance** to stay alert during these long shifts.

Gear Checklist

- Helmet
- Hood
- Goggles
- Air mask
- Air tank
- Jacket
- Gloves

- Suspenders
- Steel-toed boots
- Pants
- Flashlight
- Radio
- Ax
- Hose

Firefighters also face long-term risks. Many old buildings are made of unsafe materials. Smoke from these fires can have many **toxins**. Regular exposure to smoke and stressful work conditions increase a firefighter's risk of **heart disease** and **cancer**. Despite these risks, firefighters love their job. They will face the dangers to keep their neighbors safe!

Tragedy on the Job

On May 31, 2013, firefighters were called to a hotel and restaurant fire in Houston, Texas. Four firefighters rushed into the burning building to find trapped people. They were killed when the roof above them collapsed.

Glossary

cancer—a serious disease caused by cells that are not normal and that can spread to different parts of the body

career firefighter—a type of firefighter who works full-time for pay

collapse—to fall suddenly

endurance—the ability to do something for a long time without getting tired

fire science—the study of fire protection and firefighting techniques

first aid—emergency medical care given to a sick or injured person before he or she reaches a hospital

heart disease—any disorder that affects the heart; many people with heart disease suffer heart attacks.

inspect—to carefully examine

natural disasters—forces of nature that cause great damage; tornadoes, hurricanes, and floods are examples of natural disasters.

toxins—substances that are poisonous to humans

unconscious—not awake, especially from an injury

victim—a person who is hurt, killed, or made to suffer

volunteer—a type of firefighter who usually only works part-time for little or no pay

To Learn More

AT THE LIBRARY

Goldish, Meish. *City Firefighters.* New York, N.Y.: Bearport Publishing, 2014.

Gordon, Nick. *Smoke Jumper.* Minneapolis, Minn.: Bellwether Media, 2013.

Trammel, Howard K. *Wildfires.* New York, N.Y.: Children's Press, 2009.

ON THE WEB

Learning more about firefighters is as easy as 1, 2, 3.

1. Go to www.factsurfer.com.

2. Enter "firefighters" into the search box.

3. Click the "Surf" button and you will see a list of related web sites.

With factsurfer.com, finding more information is just a click away.

Index